He Knows My Name

Peggy K. Comer

Illustrated by Rebekah Lauzier

White Bird Publications
P.O Box 90145
Austin, Texas 78709
www.whitebirdpublications.com

Copyright©2019 by Peggy K. Comer
Illustrations by Rebekah Lauzier

ISBN: 978-1-63363-394-0
LCCN: 2019940119

ACKNOWLEDGMENT

In addition to the many ladies with whom I have studied the Bible over the last several years, I would like to recognize the following for the role they played in this journey until the publication of HE KNOWS MY NAME:

Beth and Rebekah—they mentioned the publishing company, for whom they worked, was taking submissions and did I wish to send in my poems. A special thanks to Rebekah for giving me exactly what I wanted on the cover of my book.

Evelyn, the publisher, for exceeding my expectations in her uncanny ability to size me up from a phone conversation to know exactly what would look beautiful on the pages of my book to bring out my love of pastels and flowers. She is amazing!

Ellen and Ashley Comer—my beautiful daughters-in-law who have listened to the reading of my poems and inspired me.

Grace, Andrew, Austin, Nathan, and Addison—I never knew the love that a grandmother can have for her children's children until these precious ones were born! There really is a special compartment in my heart for them that I did not know existed until their arrivals. Each one is unique and special in his/her own way.

Tim and Chris—my precious sons whom have both supported my efforts to get this book of poems published. I loved watching them grow up and into men of integrity and distinction. I truly believe they are the kindest men on the planet!

Ronnie—my husband and high school sweetheart, is definitely the "wind beneath my wings," and has always encouraged me in my writings over the years. With his words of praise, I believed I could do anything. He is a Godly husband and father, and I love him with all my heart.

Last, but certainly not least, I thank my Lord and Savior, **Jesus Christ**, who gave me such a wonderful family and network of friends. I thank Him for giving me the talent of writing down my thoughts in rhyme to glorify Him and for the enjoyment of those who read my words which were inspired from the Holy Bible.

Why were these poems written about women of old?

Writing out my thoughts and emotions in poetry is something I began doing after my brother died in 1992. I was so overwrought with sorrow in the way he lived his life and to the lonely way he died due to very low self-esteem that I had to express myself on paper. I had always been able to write out in story form my thoughts, but never had I put them to rhyme before. From that time forward, it was as if flood gates were opened, and I felt compelled to write poems for wedding showers, baby showers and births, deaths, birthdays—you name it, I loved putting my thoughts down in rhyme.

When my husband and I moved to the Longview/Hallsville area in September 2015, I desperately wanted to join a group of ladies in the church for Bible Study, but there wasn't one currently in progress. As God so often directs our paths, He opened an opportunity to begin a new study with one of my new friends and sisters in Christ. I had always admired the women of the Old and New Testaments and desired to know more about them. How different were they from the women of the 21st Century? When my friend concluded her lessons in February, she asked if I would like to lead out with a study of my choice. I quickly shared with her my desire for a study on Women of the Bible, so we began with much enthusiasm.

I believe the Bible in its original transcript is completely error-free, and that it is relevant just as much today as when it was written. Therefore, beginning with the Old Testament, we began to study the lives of the matriarchs and how they obeyed or disobeyed God. The more I studied, the more I realized those great women of God were not so different from the women of today. We have the same types of concerns in marriage, in motherhood, and in all other everyday matters. I particularly love Proverbs 31 and the description of a virtuous woman. At our meetings, we discussed the strengths and weaknesses of our woman of the week. Not long into our study, I decided to put my thoughts into poetry on each of the women we studied. The poems in this book represent my personal views of these women, and I hope those who read will feel a closer connection to them and their love of God and family. Blessings to each of you.

I chose the title of the book, "He Knows My Name," because our Lord thought it important enough to mention each one by name to make sure she received the honor and praise due her. These women had a purpose in the ministry of the Lord, and I firmly believe that each one of us today has a purpose as well.

"For I know the thoughts that I think toward you, saith the LORD, thoughts of peace and not of evil, to give you an expected end." Jeremiah 29:11

EVE

We read in the Bible of beautiful women of old,
Like Esther, whose beauty helped God's plan for His people unfold.

We know of others like Sarah, Rahab, Abigail, and Rachel so fair,
But on the sixth day of creation God, Himself, formed Eve, and none can compare.

We can only imagine how perfect they were, the first Adam, and first woman, Eve;
They were created by God's own Hand; to each other, they were to cleave.

God placed them in a garden of luscious food, fruit, and beauty.
They were supplied all they needed; tending the garden was their primary duty.

Of all the fruit of the beautiful trees only one did the Lord God deny;
The tree of knowledge of good and evil; if eaten they would surely die.

Subtler than any beast of the field, Old Satan was clever and sly;
He dared Eve to eat the forbidden fruit, and said, "You surely won't die."

Eve pondered a moment; the tree was good for food and was pleasant to her eyes;
Deceived by the serpent, she ate and gave to her husband; they both would be wise.

Sin entered the world that day, and we all fell short like this one;
But God will redeem all who believe in His only begotten Son.

"And I will put enmity between thee and the woman, and between thy seed and her seed; it
shall bruise thy head, and thou shalt bruise his heel." Genesis 3:15

SARAH

Much can be said of Sarah and her exciting, turbulent life,
But perhaps the most significant—she was a devoted, loyal wife.

God called Abraham from his native land to a place that was far away;
He said, "I will make of you a great nation; all you have to do is obey."

There were times in their travels that Abraham introduced Sarah as his sister;
She was a very beautiful woman, and the pagan kings simply could not resist her.

But God in His infinite wisdom knew their faith would waiver at times;
It was then the God of all creation would protect them from men's evil crimes.

Abraham became powerful and wealthy; respect and honor from others he won;
But years had passed, and God's promise was not fulfilled, for he had not been given a son.

Sarah's heart may have been in the right place, offering her handmaiden to Abraham one night;
But no matter how hard we justify our actions, to wait on the Lord is what's right.

Since the beginning of time from each generation, God chose a man to lead;
Seth, Noah, Shem, Abraham, Isaac, and Jacob—from them He would establish the seed.

Each of these had a partner upon whom he could always depend;
God would provide the perfect woman to be his wife and best friend.

God never breaks a promise, and to Abraham, He made it crystal clear;
Although he was 100 years old and Sarah was 90, they would have their son the next year.

So, Isaac was born to this couple, and Abraham would be the father of all nations;
His dutiful wife, the mother of all, rejoiced before God with full ululation.

As we study the women of the Bible, we learn of the good and the bad;
Some had prudence and loyalty, but some made decisions quite sad.

God's Word is relevant and important to all our everyday cares;
May we learn from our studies and heed warnings to avoid Satan's evil snares.

HAGAR
Genesis 16 & 21:1-21

She felt privileged to be the handmaid of Abram's beautiful wife;
What began as an intimate circle would end in pain and strife.

Hagar had heard the story repeated; this man had been promised of God,
He would be the Father of nations; his seed would inherit this sod.

They had dwelt ten years in Canaan, and still, no heir had been born;
As each day passed Sarah questioned her faith and became more and more forlorn.

Then much to Hagar's surprise, Sarah unveiled her new scheme;
Where once in her eyes was sadness, there was now a sparkle and gleam.

The handmaid would be given to Abram; who knows if she thought it was fair?
Taking matters into their own hands, through Hagar there would be an heir.

Hagar advanced to a stage of importance, at least in her own eyes;
She carried the child of Abram, and his wife she began to despise.

When Sarah could take it no longer, with Abram's blessing she decided the girl's fate;
She drove the maid harder and harder, in her heart was jealousy and pure hate.

When Hagar fled from their presence, the Angel of the Lord appeared in her need;
He said, "Return to your mistress, I will exceedingly multiply thy seed."

So, Ishmael was born to Abram, and he truly loved this son.
But thirteen years later with Sarah, God would give Isaac, the promised one.

When Ishmael mocked his young brother, Sarah said, "They must depart."
So, Abram sent them away, howbeit, with a grieving, broken heart.

This was not the end of the story, for once again God's Angel would appear;
Before the mother and child died of thirst in the desert, He gave news why she should not fear.

God's message to Hagar was one of hope, not despair; of her son, there would be a great nation;
When she opened her eyes, there was water; fear was replaced with pure elation.

Isaac would be the one to whom the promise was given; he would be Abram's seed;
But we read in the Bible, choices made without God's blessing, will oft cause our hearts to bleed.

THE MOTHER OF SAMSON

Known only as the wife of Manoah,
We read of this woman of old.
She found favor with the Lord in Heaven,
Whose plan for her life would unfold.

We have learned with God—nothing is impossible;
To barren women, miracles were shown.
His plans for the children of Israel
Through these women would He make known.

It happened one day while she was alone;
An angel of the Lord did appear.
He said, "You will conceive and bear a son;
It will happen within the year."

She was told to beware of wine and strong drink;
She must not eat of anything unclean.
Her son would be a Nazarite from the womb,
And would deliver them from the Philistine.

She told her husband the exciting news,
And he asked God to send the messenger once more.
He wanted to be told exactly what to do...
The angel came saying, "It is as I told your wife before."

Manoah's wife did bear a son,
And he grew and was blessed even though
He made many unwise choices,
God used him against the foe.

When all the Nazarite vows were broken
The last by the cutting of his hair;
Samson's weakness with a Philistine woman
Left him powerless and in the enemy's snare.

They put out his eyes and bound him;
He was ridiculed and displayed as a prize;
At one of the Philistines' ungodly gatherings,
Samson prayed, "Please, Lord, avenge me of my eyes."

The Lord answered Samson, whose strength was returned;
He took hold of the pillars on the left and right.
"Let me die with the Philistines." he yelled
He brought down the house with all his might.

God's ways are sometimes a mystery to us,
He uses certain people, and we may ask "WHY?"
Most important for us to remember, however;
The God of Heaven hears our earnest cry.

What must we do in an evil world?
Sins once done in darkness are now in plain sight;
As Christians we must share God's Word;
After all, we are in this world to be a "light."

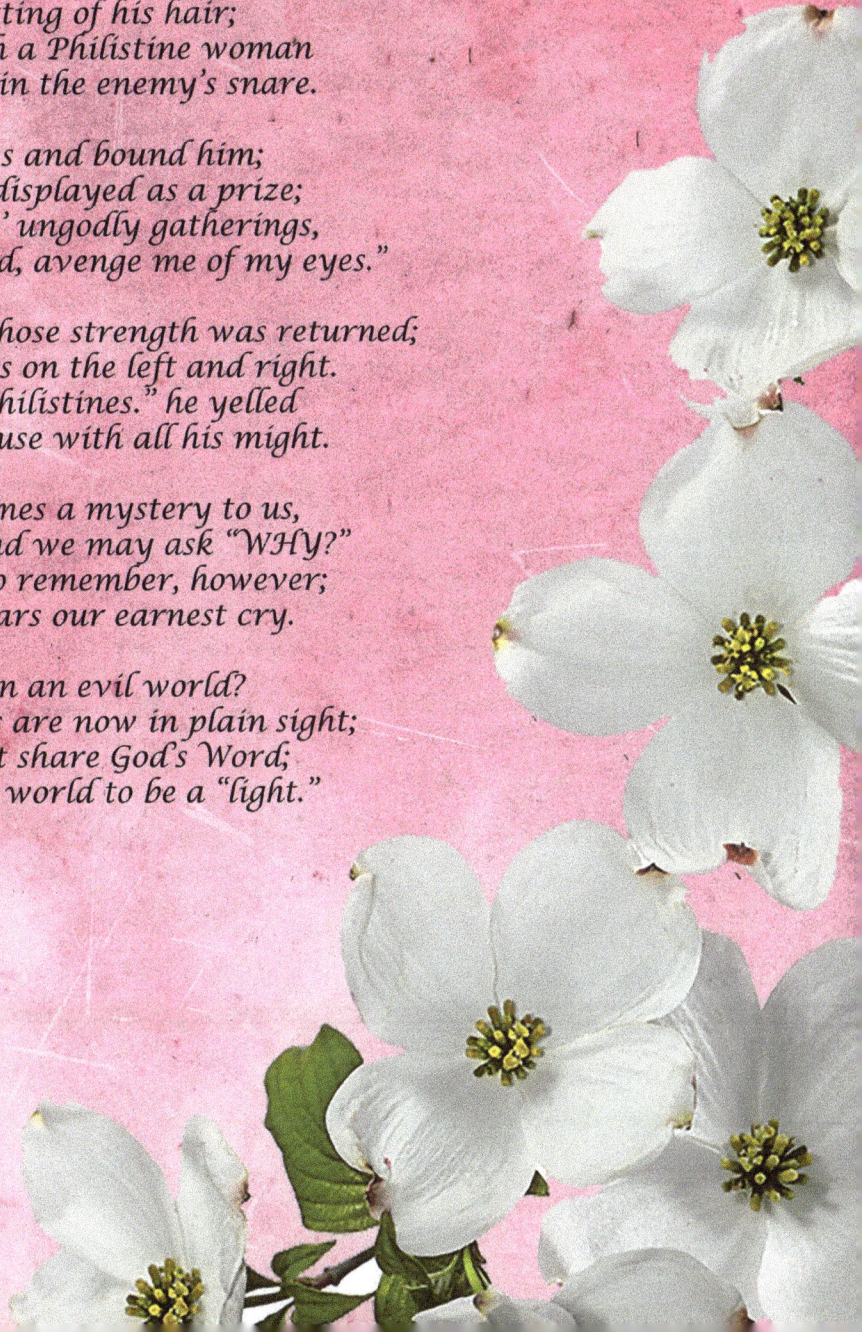

REMEMBER LOT'S WIFE

When faithful Abraham left his native country to a place he had never been,
He took his beautiful wife, Sarah, and his nephew, Lot, from among his kin.

God blessed Abraham with riches—sheep, cattle and tents galore;
But when the herdsmen began to quarrel, Lot discovered he could have even more.

To avoid strife and dissention, kind Abraham caused his nephew to rejoice;
He said, "Look at the land before us; let's separate, you may have the first choice."

Lot eyed the well-watered plains before him, and said without reservation,
"I will pitch my tent toward Sodom," a city of great wickedness and degradation.

Did Lot's wife come with him from the homeland? It is doubtful, but the Bible does not say.
Or was she a Sodomite woman? Probably, but we don't know for sure to this very day.

Not much is known of this woman, yet we are given a warning in life;
For in Luke, we are told with great consternation to "Remember Lot's wife."

She must have loved living in Sodom; the riches, the culture, the importance.
We are told it was vexing to Lot, who knew in his heart to God's will he was not in accordance.

When God decided the city was beyond saving; the people grew more evil each day.
He agreed to Abraham's question, "If there be but ten righteous, will you not destroy, I pray?"

When God's angels arrived in Sodom, they were met by Lot at the gate.
Lot urged them to stay in his home; he knew the city was filled with evil and hate.

The evil, depraved men of the city, came to Lot's house that night with ill intentions;
Attempting to dissuade them, Lot would have been killed were it not for God's intervention.

Lot was told to gather his family; they were to hurry to their new destination.
But his sons-in-law only laughed at him; scoffing at the thought of doom and devastation.

When the morning came, the angels told Lot to grab his two daughters and wife without delay;
The horrid city would be destroyed with fire and brimstone; yet lingering, they wanted to stay.

Finally, the angels knew they could wait no longer; there was no more time to waste.
Taking Lot, his wife and daughters by the hand; they left the city in great haste.

They were told to run for their lives; don't look behind and do not halt;
But Lot's wife glanced back with longing, and she was turned to a pillar of salt.

RUTH

To escape a famine, they fled to my country of Moab; this Israelite family of four.
They brought with them in their life-style, strange beliefs, and customs galore.

When Elimelech died, the two sons remained, with their mother consumed with grief.
All would be fine; the boys would marry, grandchildren would come…this was her belief.

I considered myself blessed to be chosen by one son, and Orpah by the other;
We were told about their Israelite God, their faith we did discover.

Orpah and I learned so much from Naomi, who was kind and treated us as her own.
Then tragedy struck, and both brothers are dead; just like that, three widows left all alone.

Naomi was heart-broken; I had never seen her this way. To her homeland, she would return.
We will go with you, we pledged to her; the depth of her sorrow not hard to discern.

Orpah turned back; we were both so young; we had our whole lives ahead of us.
But steadfastly, I refused to return to false gods, for in the God of Israel I had come to trust.

When we finally arrived in Bethlehem-Judah, the city was all astir.
Could this be Elimelech's widow, Naomi? Could this really be her?

It was the beginning of barley harvest; did Naomi know? I really cannot say.
We were destitute and discouraged for sure, but God would show us the way.

I gleaned in the fields of a man named Boaz who was kind and respectful to me.
"This man is our kinsman." Naomi exclaimed, "Things will work out. You will see."

I followed a plan that Naomi lined out, laying my fears aside.
Boaz became the love of my life; under his protection, we both would abide.

Now the story of Ruth is told and re-told of the remarkable part she would play;
In the lineage and ancestry of the Son of God, whose body on the cross would lay.

Along with Naomi, Boaz, Obed, Jesse, and David, Ruth's heart eternally sings.
For hallelujah, and glory to God, she met Jesus, the King of Kings.

"…Entreat me not to leave thee, or to return from following after thee: for whither thou goest,
I will go; and where thou lodgest, I will lodge: thy people shall be my people,
and thy God my God…" Ruth 1:16

BATHSHEBA
2 Samuel 11 & 12

She had just finished bathing on a beautiful, warm night
When a knock at her door caused her to fright.

There in the doorway was a messenger from the King.
He desired her presence...what could this mean?

Why wasn't the king fighting with the other men of might?
She hurriedly got dressed; what an extraordinary night.

Upon her arrival, it became crystal clear...
The great king of Israel desired HER...Oh dear.

Does she have a say in the matter? What is taking place?
Thoughts of Uriah flooded her mind—she could see his kind face.

A man of God, King David was known;
Could she dare say no to the man on the throne?

As His Word tells us, God cannot be deceived;
As a result of this encounter, a child was conceived.

Although this was a problem, he could not easily dismiss,
King David would bring the soldier home; the child would be his.

Because of Uriah's loyalty to his God and the throne;
He could not be convinced to return to his home.

To Joab a message was given that could not be mistaken;
The life of this valiant servant would have to be taken.

After mourning her husband, David took her as his wife;
But sin has consequences—his reign in the kingdom would forever have strife.

David repented, and his sin was forgiven;
But the boy child born to them would not stay among the living.

The moral of this story of which there is no exemption;
God sent His Son to the cross to provide for redemption.

"If we confess our sins, He is faithful and just to forgive us our sins,
and to cleanse us from all unrighteousness." 1 John 1:9

JEHOSHEBA
2 Chronicles 22 - 24

We learn from the Bible of kings both evil and good;
Their destinies were determined upon whose side they stood.

If they stood with God and the prophets and chose to obey,
God was faithful to show them the right way.

Jehosheba was the wife of a priest who remained faithful and true,
When wicked Athaliah was murdering the king's sons, she knew what to do.

Risking her life, she hid the king's infant son in the temple six years long;
And in the seventh year, her brave husband, Jehoiada rose up mighty and strong.

It is not right that an illegitimate queen should claim power as her own;
Joash, the king's son, though only a child, should sit on the throne.

The Messiah would come from the seed of David; the prophesy had been given;
A new plan was formed, and now was the time. From the throne, she must be driven.

We pay tribute to Jehosheba for her role in God's plan; to make Joash the king;
God uses women to accomplish His will, and His praises we continue to sing.

What if no one was willing to step up and speak against evil in high power?
We thank God for those faithful ones who determined in their presence not to cower.

This account in the Bible seems almost obscure, but its message is still true today;
Much is accomplished as the women of God gain knowledge and remember to pray.

2 Peter 3:9 "The Lord is not slack concerning His promise, as some men count slackness; but is longsuffering to us-ward, not willing that any should perish, but that all should come to repentance."

ESTHER

A young woman of stunning beauty, Esther lived in Persia but was of Jewish birth.
Mordecai had come up with an idea; the craziest thing she had heard on earth.

The arrogant Persian King Ahasuerus, from his kingdom had banished the queen;
And now he was looking to replace her, but he was known to be spiteful and mean.

Now Esther was beholden to her cousin with an undying loyalty so strong.
When orphaned, he stepped in as her father and would never ask her to do anything wrong.

She would go to the palace as summoned, along with other young virgins as well.
She would go through the purifying process; that she was Jewish, she would not tell.

The chamberlain assigned to the virgins, to bring out their most beautiful feature,
Took an instant liking to Esther, who was an exquisite and lovely creature.

When it was Esther's time to go before the king, he was mesmerized when he saw her face;
There was no need to look any further; she filled the room with beauty and grace.

Haman was a man of great power, and for the Jews, he was filled with hate.
Mordecai would not bow down before him; his defiance was known publicly at the gate.

As retribution Haman convinced the king to issue a decree - the Jews he would destroy;
Mordecai hastily notified Esther of the plot, for her help he wished to employ.

After fasting and praying for deliverance, Esther came up with a plan of her own.
If she found favor with the king once more, her ancestry would she make known.

Learning the events that had happened, the king was angry and had to get a breath of fresh air.
Returning, he saw Haman pleading his cause, and he ordered his hanging right then and there.

Esther's courage to stand up for God's people, when her very own life was at stake,
Inspires us all to have faith in God and to pray before any decisions we make.

"...and who knoweth whether thou art cometh to the kingdom for such a time as this." Esther 4:14

ELISABETH
Luke 1

There lived in the days of Herod, the king,
Zacharias, a beloved and honorable priest.
His wife, Elisabeth, was of the daughters of Aaron,
Righteous before God, their love for Him daily increased.

They had no children, for Elisabeth was barren;
And now they were well stricken in years.
When she looked upon children with love in her heart,
She would often resort to tears.

While Zacharias performed priestly duties in the temple;
An angel appeared with a message hard to believe.
He announced that the Lord had heard their prayers,
And Elisabeth would, at appointed time, conceive.

He was told they would have a beautiful child,
Much rejoicing would occur at the birth of a son.
He would be special and sent from God,
Said the angel, "His name shall be called John."

Well, this news was simply too much for this elderly priest.
And he blurted out that he and his wife were too old.
Because of his unbelief, he would not be able to speak,
Until the prophecy was fulfilled just as the angel had told.

When Elisabeth was in her sixth month with child,
Another miracle and prophecy would unfold.
Upon Mary's greeting, Elisabeth's babe leaped inside her
The world's Greatest Love Story was about to be told.

Elisabeth was filled with the Holy Ghost,
And she shouted with happiness and glee;
"Blessed are thou among women," she said,
"The mother of my Lord has come to me."

"There was a man sent from God, whose name was John. The same came for a witness, to bear witness of the Light that all men through Him might believe." John 1:6-7

MARY, THE MOTHER OF JESUS

God had been silent for four-hundred years, not even one word from the Father;
But Mary's parents taught their daughter the scriptures, though others said, "Why bother?"

This devout Jewish family believed what the prophets had said, and in their hearts, they knew,
The God of Abraham, Isaac, Jacob, and David would do what He said He would do.

He promised a Messiah would come one day and be born of a virgin girl;
When this young Jewish maid of Nazareth had a visit from the angel, her mind began to swirl.

Little by little Scriptures fell into place, and she and Joseph were revealed the plan;
The Holy Ghost would overshadow Mary, and she would give birth to the Son of Man.

Her barren cousin, Elisabeth, would also be blessed with the birth of a baby boy;
In perfect obedience and love in her heart, Mary visited to share their JOY.

Blessed among women, she was called that day and has been honored throughout history;
And blessed are we who believe God's Word, which fully explains this mystery.

What a wonderful honor to be chosen to be the Mother of God's Holy Son.
How awesome for this young peasant girl to give birth to the Messiah, the Promised One.

We know the story of the shepherds and the angels who sang at His birth
Glory to God in the highest, and good tidings and peace on the earth.

Thirty-three years had passed, and Mary marveled at the intelligence and powers of her Son;
He healed the sick, caused the blind to see, and the lame to walk again—without sin, no not one.

When Jesus was nailed to the old rugged cross, to die for the sins of the entire world;
Mary's heart was breaking amid the shouts of "Crucify Him," among the insults being hurled.

He was lied about, spat upon, cursed and betrayed by the kiss of one He called friend;
Though prophecy was being fulfilled, it most assuredly was not the end.

Her faith renewed, her heart beamed with pride when He arose on the third day as her Savior;
And true to the Holy Word, to this very day, we honor Mary found to be in God's favor.

"And the angel came in unto her, and said, Hail, thou that art highly favoured, the Lord is with thee:
blessed art thou among women." Luke 1:28

ANNA AND SIMEON
Luke 2: 25-38

Old Anna shuffled along on familiar floors tiled,
When she heard the soft cry of a little child.

She looked ahead to a scene unfolding,
Old Simeon, a baby in his arms was holding.

With excitement, she stepped up her usual snail's pace,
For pure wonder and joy shone on the old man's face.

In their frequent discussions from the prophets of old,
And recent claims from the shepherds; it had all been foretold.

The Holy Ghost was upon this old man, just and devout;
Now Anna must hurry to see what was coming about.

To God be the Glory on this wondrous occasion.
His old eyes had witnessed Israel's consolation.

Now he could go to his eternal destination;
God kept His promise; he had seen the salvation.

The young mother marveled as the news took its toll;
Simeon told her a sword would pierce her own soul.

Now Anna, the prophetess, gave thanks likewise;
She would speak to all who looked for the Savior and Christ.

This aged widow and Simeon had prayed night and day;
They would both be remembered for what they each had to say.

What a blessing is ours and truly without measure;
We find in God's Word the world's greatest treasure.

We are called upon as Christians to share what we believe;
For by grace are ye saved through faith; God's greatest gift— RECEIVE.

THE WOMAN WITH AN ISSUE OF BLOOD
Mark 5: 25-34

Breathlessly and painfully, she forged ahead;
Working her way through the crowd,
Praying she would go unnoticed;
For if seen, she would not be allowed.

She had heard of the miracles He had done;
Of the various healings and such.
In her heart was the belief she, too, could be helped;
If only His garment she could touch.

She was an outcast, and had been for years;
Unclean just as everyone had said...
Twelve years had gone by, and lonely, she was;
Desperate and broke, her body still bled.

Just as she thought she could not go on,
Body aching from her head to her toes,
She dared look up and saw she had made it.
She reached out and touched His clothes.

In the moment her hand touched His garment,
Just that quick, her body became like new.
Deep in her heart was instant rejoicing -
What she had heard of Him was true.

Much to her horror, He turned around;
And asked who had touched His clothes.
The disciples wondered among themselves,
With this multitude of people, who knows?

With fear and much trembling,
But with a body made new,
She fell before Him,
Not knowing what He would do.

He called her Daughter, an endearing term.
Eyes filled with mercy and grace.
"Thy faith has made thee whole," He said,
"You are free. Go in peace from this place."

THE SYRO-PHOENICIAN WOMAN
Matthew 15: 21-28 and Mark 7: 24-30

A mother's heart can generate a love toward her child that makes her resourceful and bold;
The Bible tells of a Syro-Phoenician woman whose daughter was vexed by a devil of old.

This woman had heard of the prophet from Galilee and that His powers were beyond belief;
Without hesitation, she decided to seek Him for her precious daughter's relief.

This child was spastic and wild with her actions—eyes filled with terror and fear.
This mother would seek the one whom she had heard about; He was in the city so near.

She cried out to Him, "Oh Lord. Son of David. Please have mercy on me.
My daughter is grievously vexed with a demon." Those nearby would hear her plea.

Jesus answered not a word, and the disciples said, "Master, should we send her away?"
But she, being full of faith and worship, said, "Oh no, Lord, please help me, I pray."

Now Jesus was the Son of God, and His Father's plan must be done;
He was sent first to the House of Israel; for now, they were number one.

But how could He refuse this woman? His explanation fell on deaf ears much like a fable.
She had said that even the dogs ate the crumbs that fell from their master's table.

This woman had addressed Him as Lord, and the son of David as well;
Compassion filled our Lord and Savior, as He saw the tears in her eyes begin to swell.

He had not seen faith as great as this; much less from a pagan soul.
He said, "Return to your home, from this hour your daughter has been made whole."

Jesus went forth from that place to a mountain by the Sea of Galilee;
Multitudes came with the lame and the blind to the One who could make them free.

Jesus performed many miracles in His day, and His Father received the Glory;
Today we are still reading the accounts; we are learning from every story.

As women today, we can learn from the Word of God just what to do and say;
We will spread the Good News, open our hearts to others, and we will never cease to pray.

"But without faith it is impossible to please Him; for he that cometh to God must believe that He is, and that He is a rewarder of them that diligently seek Him." Hebrews 11:6

SALOME
Matthew 20:20-28

Salome was the Christian Mother of James and John, the sons of Zebedee;
She was likely the sister of the Mother of Jesus, whom, when small, probably sat on her knee.

While Jesus walked and taught on the earth of His coming kingdom and reign,
Salome listened intently and understood He was the Messiah, and her faith was not in vain.

She was proud of her sons, and rightly so, for she was a Godly mother;
She once asked Jesus when He sat on the throne, could her sons sit on one side and the other.

Jesus did not scold this faithful follower for her ignorant but innocent request;
He simply said she did not know what she was asking; His Father would do what was best.

They would indeed share in His suffering for Jesus knew of events coming up fast;
Of the apostles, James would be the first martyr, and John would be the last.

The other disciples were indignant and angry that this mother and sons would be so bold;
Although each of them had wished the same thing, if the truth had been told.

To be rebuked in the presence of so many, Salome could have reacted in a different way;
She could withdraw her presence, wealth, and influence, but by Jesus' side, she decided to stay.

When Jesus hung on the old rugged cross, Salome clung to Mary and her strong, loving son;
She would hear the words of Jesus when He commended His mother to the beloved John.

Over two thousand years have gone by, and yet the story is vivid as it is told and re-told;
And to think this passage was included for our learning about this faithful woman of old.

May we honor the tradition of our Godly mothers; may we study and learn from the best;
As we go about our daily lives, leading others to Christ should be our quest.

"They that sow in tears shall reap in joy. He that goeth forth and weepeth,
bearing precious seed, shall doubtless come again with rejoicing,
bringing his sheaves with him." Psalm 126: 5-6

MARY MAGDALENE
Luke 8:2 and Mark 15: 40-47

Vexed and controlled by demons, seven in all, was this woman, Mary Magdalene;
Imagine her incredible joy, when from that prison,
she was delivered by Jesus, the Nazarene.

How could she show her gratitude? What in the world could she do?
She would leave all behind and follow her King ministering with a heart so true.

She witnessed the miracles; the compassion and love as He walked upon the earth;
She heard the stories straight from His mother of the Messiah's amazing birth.

Despite His power and healing words, Jewish leaders wanted Him dead.
They did not think twice when He could have been freed; they chose Barabbas instead.

As He hung on the cross, a small band of women stood as close as they could nearby;
They watched in sorrow each anguishing moment; they heard every moan and cry.

They would not leave Him. He would see their devotion as they witnessed the prophecy doom;
How reassuring it was to witness Joseph of Arimathea as he offered his own new tomb.

Bright and early that first Easter morning, Mary Magdalene
rushed to where her Savior was laid; Jesus had been wrapped in linen
and laid in the tomb, but more preparation had been made.

To her great surprise, the tomb was empty, and her Lord had been taken away.
But wait. Hallelujah! He had arisen! Oh my, what a glorious day...

Upon hearing her name, she trembled with astonishment and joy. Share the hope.
She would be the first messenger of the risen Lord. The disciples had no reason to mope.

Were you there when they crucified my Lord? These words of a song come to mind.
She was last at the cross and first at the tomb. One more loyal than Mary, we will not find.

May we rise as women and answer His call; may we have a servant's heart.
May those who come behind us find us faithful; in service to the Master, may we do our part.

"Then said Jesus unto them, Be not afraid: go tell my brethren that they go into Galilee,
and there shall they see me." Matthew 28:10

MARTHA
Luke 10: 38-42 and John 11: 1-46

Martha was considered a wonderful hostess; she entertained Jesus and His disciples in style.
She could clean the entire house, cook a fine meal, and serve it all up with a smile.

She lived with her siblings, Lazarus and Mary, whom she loved with all her heart;
Now Jesus had come, and Martha was busy serving, but Mary was not doing her part.

Martha had cleaned and cooked and was serving the guests while Mary was nowhere in sight;
When Martha found her, she was sitting at the feet of Jesus. Now surely that was not right.

"Jesus," she said, "don't you care that my sister has left me to do the serving all alone?"
"Martha, thou art troubled about many things," Jesus answered with kindness in His tone.

"Your sister, Mary, chooses to hear my word; she is hiding it in her heart.
Time will come when you look back on this day and will see Mary has chosen the good part."

Jesus loved these friends and knew He could count on them whenever He was in need;
One day He received word from the sisters, "Our brother is sick, come quickly." they did plead.

But Jesus waited a couple of days, and then headed out, for He knew what He would do.
The disciples tried to get Him to stay where He was; they had not a clue.

The mourners had come; Lazarus was dead and in the grave four days;
But Martha ran to meet Jesus when she heard He was coming; her mind was in a haze.

"If only you had been here, Lord, my brother would not have died.
We let you know in plenty of time. Why did you tarry?" she cried.

When Jesus said to Martha, "Your brother will rise again," she responded in sweet reflection;
"You are the Christ, the Son of God, and I believe my brother will be in the resurrection."

She tried to tell Mary in secret Jesus had come, but when they left the house in a hurry,
The mourners and Jews whom had gathered with them followed in quite a scurry.

Couldn't this one have done something? He had given sight to the blind and healed the lame;
They watched in amazement as He said, "Lazarus, come forth." and out of the grave he came.

Many believed on Jesus this day, and Martha and Mary had a part in this story.
We, too, can follow Martha's and Mary's lead, and our lives can reflect God's Glory.

SWEET MARY OF BETHANY
Luke 10:38-42 and John 12: 1-9

Mary was oblivious of her surroundings that day; she had only one thing on her mind;
Jesus was visiting, and sitting at His feet, she listened to His words intriguing and kind.

Martha, her dear sister with whom she lived, was hustling and bustling about;
Much cumbered with serving, she promptly asked Jesus to tell Mary to please help her out.

Jesus was kind with His words to Martha, but He told her for little things she should not worry;
I couldn't help but think of how we live our lives today—aren't we always in a "hurry?"

We don't make the time to be still and listen to God, and His wonderful words of life;
Instead, we scurry from here to there, beneath loads of worry and strife.

Mary took a rare and cherished spikenard that was both expensive and dear;
Pouring it on Jesus' feet, the full meaning would soon become clear.

Mary had listened to the words of her Lord, and she must have known in her heart;
The death of her Savior and Lord was coming, and toward His burial, she was doing her part.

Judas Iscariot criticized this act and asked why it wasn't sold for money and given to the needy;
This he asked not because he was lofty and noble, but because he was a thief and greedy.

Jesus let everyone know that day that sweet Mary of Bethany had a heart of gold;
This act would be spoken of often, and centuries later, it is still being told.

Do we want to be like Martha and Mary? Each differing in their service to the Lord...
May our hearts and minds be refreshed, and may we live our lives in His will and accord.

"Then said Jesus, let her alone: against the day of my burying hath she kept this.
For the poor always ye have with you; but me ye have not always." John 12: 7-8

THE WOMAN AT THE WELL
(The Samaritan Woman) John 4

It was just around noon that eventful day,
As she walked down the path all alone.
Preferring this task in the cool of the morning with others;
She simply wasn't welcome; a fact well known.

Because of poor choices she had made in life,
Their kind of friendship could never mix;
She had been married five times after all,
And now was living with number six.

She approached the well for water that day,
And a Jewish man stood nearby.
For him to be traveling through Samaria,
Was a custom he chose to defy.

He looked a little weary and tired,
For the sun above was blasting.
Although He asked for a drink, it was actually He
Who offered water that would give life everlasting.

After listening intently for just a while,
She knew He wasn't the one needing a favor;
Could He be the one she had heard about?
Could He be the Messiah, the Savior?

What joy. What love. He knew all about her.
And He loved her without consternation;
Leaving her water pot behind, she quickly departed
To tell all she knew of this revelation.

Because of her testimony, many were saved that day.
And even more when, to Jesus, they came.
He was invited to speak and to share the gospel with them,
And the lives of these Samaritans would never be the same.

Could we be so bold a witness as she?
Could we tell others about this great treasure?
The answer is YES, for we are commanded,
And the benefits are far beyond measure.

RHODA
Acts 12: 1-17

As Peter in prison between two guards lay shackled,
He slept with a strange sense of sweet peace.
Normally easily agitated, tonight he just prayed;
He knew only a miracle would secure his release.

Not far away in the home of John Mark,
Rhoda quietly walked among the saints gathered there.
She had seen to their needs, and could retire if she wished;
But instead, she chose to join them in prayer.

Herod, the king, had stretched forth his hands,
To vex the church and cause them discord.
When he saw it pleased many of the Jews,
He had the apostle James killed with a sword.

And now, Peter, was imprisoned with sixteen soldiers,
It appeared he, too, would suffer the same fate.
When Rhoda heard a knock at the door,
She wondered who could be coming so late.

A voice cried out, "Hurry, open the door;
If they find me, I'll surely be killed."
Rhoda was stunned when she heard Peter's voice,
And her heart could have not been more thrilled.

Rushing inside to tell the others the news,
She shouted that Peter stood at the gate.
Rising from bended knees, they thought she was mad.
They noticed the time, and it was awfully late.

When she insisted they come and look for themselves,
They figured Peter had surely met his demise.
Then, they too heard the insistent knocking,
And they could hardly believe their eyes.

Peter hurriedly told them exactly what happened;
An angel had led him out with a touch.
The fervent, effectual prayers of believers;
Had most definitely availed much.

PHOEBE
Romans 16:1-2

Not much is told about Phoebe, but she is mentioned by her very own name;
Paul especially held her in high esteem; in God's Word, she has recognition and fame.

We know she was a Greek Gentile, saved by God's amazing grace;
Her name means "pure and radiant as the moon," the light of Jesus was upon her face.

Paul loved her as a sister; she was a servant of the church;
She was always ready to assist him and would never leave him in a lurch.

When Paul wrote a letter to the Romans, he entrusted it with Phoebe to get there;
He wanted the church at Rome to know he loved them and for his visit to prepare.

The Christians at Rome were both Jew and Gentile; he loved them all very much.
He also wanted them to know they were not forgotten; he wanted to stay in touch.

Paul commended to them, Phoebe, his sister, and servant in sharing the good news;
He asked them to receive her with Christ-like manner; he knew they would not refuse.

He asked them to accept her, and to assist her in any way she needed;
After all, she had been a helper to others; Paul was sure his request would be heeded.

We are told that God's Word was inspired by Him—and nothing is there by chance.
Therefore, we must believe this mention of Phoebe is for our lives to enhance.

As women, we sometimes feel insignificant; as if our lives don't really matter;
But what joy we find in the pages of the Bible when we get away from the noise and chatter.

As we search the Scriptures for nuggets of wisdom and answers to all of life's fear;
We see He has a purpose for each one of us; as we study, it all becomes clear.

May we become stronger, more faithful and courageous as we learn from the women of old;
It's obvious from all the examples, we do not all fit in the same mold.

I present to you a challenge—study God's Word, so you will not lack;
As we look at the events that have already happened, rest assured He is coming back.

"...sanctify the Lord God in your hearts: and be ready always to give an answer to every man that asketh
you a reason of the hope that is in you with meekness and fear." 1 Peter 3:15

PRISCILLA

Acts 18; Romans 16:3; 1 Corinthians 16:19; 2 Timothy 4:19

Priscilla was married to Aquila, and in scripture they are never mentioned alone;
This Roman couple, tentmakers, and believers in Christ knew how to set the right tone.

Forced to leave Rome, this Jewish couple moved to Corinth and continued making their tents;
When Paul arrived, he stayed in their home; as a tentmaker himself, it made perfect sense.

Imagine the conversations they would have each night as they rejoiced in God's blessings;
The Gospel was being taught every single day, and in Jesus Christ, there were many confessing.

When Paul journeyed on to Ephesus, this Godly couple was right by his side;
But when Paul departed, Priscilla and Aquila stayed behind in God's Will to abide.

A certain Jew, named Apollos, eloquent and mighty, knowing only the baptism of John;
Spoke boldly in the synagogue, and Priscilla and Aquila expounded to him the more perfect One.

They took him aside, and in a Christ-like way shared Jesus, God's only Son;
Apollos was a powerful preacher, and through his ministry, many souls for Christ were won.

Priscilla was truly a woman of God, one whom we all can admire in her Christian life;
We learn in God's Word, she was faithful and loyal—a devoted and loving wife.

Paul would always give thanks for Priscilla and Aquila, and they would be mentioned by name;
They had risked their own lives for him, and in the Lord's work, they would forever have fame.

Once again in God's Word, we are given an example of a marriage close to God's heart;
This couple loved each other dearly; they loved God's people; they were happy to do their part.

This couple labored together; their hearts beat as one as they served their precious Lord;
They are known for their devotion, love, and affection—working in one accord.

According to the martyr-ology of the Roman Church, and if what is recorded in history is right;
They both were beheaded together: we can say they truly fought the "good fight."

"And let us not be weary in well doing: for in due season
we shall reap if we faint not." Galatians 6:9

LOIS AND EUNICE
Acts 16:1-3; 2 Timothy 1:5 & 2 Timothy 3:14-17

Timothy was a blessed little boy whose mother and grandmother were Jews;
Although his father was an unbelieving Greek, his mother's faith he would choose.

Eunice and Lois thought it imperative to teach the youngster God's Word so true;
Before Paul arrived, the Old Testament Scriptures, however, were all that they knew.

When that great Missionary Paul arrived in Lystra one glorious, eventful day,
Lois and Eunice listened with joy and accepted Jesus as the "One and only way."

From that point on, they would teach the gospel to the precious little son;
Paul rejoiced with them when through God's Word, this young heart would be won.

Young Timothy, with unfeigned faith, would travel and learn from Missionary Paul,
Only God knows the number of souls he would lead to Christ because he answered the call.

When Paul was imprisoned, deserted by others, he wrote young Timothy a letter;
His time on earth would soon be over and seeing his "son in the faith" would make him better.

This beautiful epistle was written to Timothy to encourage him in the work of the Lord;
Thankful for his unfeigned faith, dwelling first in his mother and grandmother in sweet accord.

We are told in this passage all scripture is inspired of God and is profitable in all ways;
We should learn and keep it close to our hearts and share it with others all our days.

We live in a world where everyone is busy and won't take time in God's presence to rest;
But praying and Bible reading at bedtime would help children be spiritually blessed.

Great men of old have always proclaimed the influence of their mothers;
We pay tribute today to Eunice and Lois, and the effect their faith had on so many others.

"Train up a child in the way he should go, and when he is old,
he will not depart from it." Proverbs 22:6

LYDIA, SELLER OF PURPLE
Acts 16:9-15 & 40

Led by the Spirit to Troas, Paul was told to Macedonia he must carry,
The Gospel of Jesus Christ, and he must hurry, for there was no time to tarry.

Paul was to present the good news to the Gentiles, and to Europe he must go;
There were people there whose hearts were ready the Messiah to know.

When he set foot on the shore of Neapolis, a seaport on the Macedonian coast;
His first convert was Lydia, seller of purple, a businesswoman who would become a great host.

In a day when women had little distinction, this one would stand tall and shine;
Skilled in the dyes and textiles; her colors were crimson & purple, gorgeous and fine.

Lydia was beautiful and elegant; she wore her fabrics with dignity and ease;
It would not be hard to imagine the influence and ability her clients to please.

Did she sell her bolts of purple to the wealthy and perhaps to the Jewish priest?
Were her products found in the temple draperies? Or in their vestments at the very least?

We can glean from the Holy Scriptures; this woman was used by the Lord with grace;
She would answer the call to salvation, and in pages of history, she would take her place.

When Paul, Luke, Timothy, and Silas went to the riverside meeting place;
To their surprise, just a few women were gathered there to hear of God's amazing grace.

Paul knew that he was sent there by the Holy Spirit, so he preached Jesus crucified.
Lydia listened intently, and the longing and searching of her heart was finally satisfied.

That day she became a believer, and she would give of her earthly treasure;
She would entertain Paul and his friends—her gift of hospitality was of great measure.

She and her family were baptized, and she would spend the rest of her days;
Serving the Lord with gladness; of His goodness, she would continually praise.

She would be the first European convert and would share His Word every day.
Lydia would be known in the Church of Philippi as a woman who knew how to pray.

Can we rise and be counted with those who are known for a servant's heart?
May our Father, who is in Heaven, bless us with revival. He has equipped us to do our part.

"I can do all things through Christ which strengtheneth me." Philippians 4:13

HERODIAS AND HER DAUGHTER
Matthew 14:1-12

Herodias was the mother of Salome, and her life has us all appalled.
"The Jezebel of the New Testament," is most often what she is called.

I hesitated to write a poem about her; I didn't want to give her any acclaim.
However, our Lord thought it significant to mention her, so I will do the same.

She was the granddaughter of Herod the Great who was known as an evil one.
He had his favorite wife murdered, her brothers, and even his very own son.

A descendant of Esau, Herodias knew a heritage of selfishness and greed.
If only she had listened to the words of John the Baptist; if only she had taken heed.

She was married to Herod Philip, and they had a daughter not quite grown.
Her husband held lots of power, and they made their home in Rome.

Herod Antipas had more power than his brother, Philip, and Herodias was drawn in.
The two developed an attraction to each other, and adultery was their sin.

It soon became evident, that the two made a pretty good match;
He had more power than Philip, and Herodias thought he would be a good catch.

They each left their spouses and lived their lives full of selfishness and greed.
Confess and repent of your sin, John the Baptist to them would plead.

Often, he would remind them of their sin, but his words were of no avail.
To appease his wife, Herod Antipas had John the Baptist hauled off to jail.

At his drunken birthday party, Herod was pleased by his step daughter's lewd dance.
Wanting to please her, as well, he offered her a gift, and she knew this would be her chance.

She asked her mother for what she should ask and was shocked at what she said.
The wicked Herodias didn't think twice; on a platter she wanted the Baptist's head.

Herod was weak and could not say no; after all, he had pledged in front of his peers.
He called for the terrible deed to be carried out, dismissing his mounting fears.

If Salome's mother had been like Timothy's, God's Word she would often reflect.
Sadly, she was unrepentant and the most important thing in life, she would choose to reject.

THE WIDOW WITH TWO MITES

Jesus often taught in the temple and reasoned with the scribes of the day.
When asked to comment on controversial subjects, He responded in a skillful way.

In desperate attempts they tried to trip Him up...Should they pay tribute to Caesar or refuse?
What is the first and greatest commandment? Of the others can we pick and choose?

The Sadducees asked about the resurrection; the widow of seven husbands in her life;
When she dies and goes to heaven, of which one will she be the wife?

From the image on the coin and superscription, Jesus said to pay Caesar his due.
The first commandment gives God all glory and honor, and to Him be loyal and true

It was ironic coming from the Sadducees, "Of which husband would she be the wife?"
Especially since this sect of the Jews did not believe in the after-life.

It was just such a day in the temple when Jesus answered questions left and right.
He called the disciples together and told of the widow's mites.

The wealthy paraded around in the treasury with looks that were superior and proud;
They dropped in coins of their abundance feeling certain they would "wow" the crowd.

The widow in poverty quietly dropped in her two coins with a heart so full and glad.
Jesus pointed out that she had given more than the others, for she had given all she had.

She had entered the temple with two coins to her name and would give them to God that day.
Trusting in His Word her needs would be met; this faithful woman surely knew how to pray.

Although we do not read more of this precious soul, I believe she was taken care of;
After all, Jesus, the Messiah had memorialized her with admiration and love.

Perhaps the Lord has not asked of us to give all we have on this earth;
But He surely expects us to give with cheer in our hearts – a sign of our spiritual birth.

"But my God shall supply all your need according to His riches in glory by Christ Jesus."
Philippians 4:19

"Every man according as he purposeth in his heart, so let him give; not grudgingly, or of necessity: for
God loveth a cheerful giver." 2 Corinthians 9:7

DAMARIS
Acts 17

God directs the paths of His children, and He surely ordered the steps of Paul;
Chased out of Thessalonica and Berea, to Athens, he would answer God's call.

Deeply troubled by the wickedness and idolatry there, Paul had to have his say.
God sent him to witness to everyone, so he preached the gospel that very day.

Among the people who heard him speak were philosophers and the curious;
Many thought he was a babbler; others mocked and thought him not serious.

But as we know, God's Word never returns void; it is always powerful and true.
The Gospel was proclaimed that day, and Damaris, believing, knew what to do.

She was one of many who had assembled on Mars Hill to hear of a doctrine new;
Athenians were known for their love of learning, so gathered were more than a few.

It took a lot of courage for a woman of that day, and especially in Athens, Greece.
But through faith, she accepted Christ; and her idol worship would instantly cease.

Was Damaris a woman of prominence? Was she known to be noble and smart?
One thing is clear, she walked away that day with a pure and cleansed heart.

Maybe you know someone who appears to be above your intellect or class;
Just remember, God's Word does the work, don't let your moment pass.

Sometimes we are called upon to speak for the Lord, so please do not fret;
Pray for courage, strength, and conviction; Jesus Christ has paid our debt.

"For God so loved the world, that He gave His only begotten Son,
that whosoever believeth in Him should not perish, but have everlasting life." John 3:16

DORCAS
Acts 9: 36-42

Dorcas was a doer of the Word, of which she did not boast;
She was called a disciple from Joppa, a city on the coast.

She lived up to the "woman of virtue," described in Proverbs thirty-one;
Stretching out her hand to the poor and needy, thanks and appreciation expecting none.

Her Greek name was Dorcas; in Hebrew, Tabitha, which means gazelle;
A beautiful, graceful antelope with glowing eyes deep and shining as a well.

This Jewish woman lived among the Greeks, her generosity well known by all;
She sewed for the widows and orphans, garments for the big and the small

Living so close to the sea, Dorcas knew of the many shipwrecks and sorrow;
The families that once had a husband and father, might now have to beg and borrow.

This kind woman knew of her calling; she would use her gift for God's Glory.
She would sew new garments and repair some old ones; the Book of Acts tells her story.

When Dorcas became sick and died; hearts all over the city were broken;
Widows gathered at her home wearing garments she had made; thankful words quietly spoken.

Peter at nearby Lydda, was summoned to come quickly to comfort in their time of need.
This beautiful, kind and loving woman was gone. God's healing and mercy, they would plead

When Peter arrived in Joppa, he went to the upper chamber where Dorcas was laid;
The widows lovingly showed him the garments... this saintly woman for them had made.

Touched by the love and concern of the mourners speaking softly and milling about;
Peter with his unflinching faith in the power of the Risen Lord, asked them all to go out.

Peter kneeled and prayed, then turned to her lifeless body and said, "Tabitha, arise."
To God be the Glory! It was surely a miracle! Dorcas opened her eyes!

This news was known throughout all Joppa, throughout the region there was fame;
And just as the Lord had ordained it, many believed on Jesus' name.

We may not can sew garments for the poor, and our God-given gifts may vary;
But as we learn from the Scriptures, the Lord made miracles from the "plain and ordinary."

"She seeketh wool, and flax, and worketh willingly with her hands."
Proverbs 31:13

OLD TESTAMENT WOMEN IN REVIEW

Eve was the first woman, beautiful and perfect - formed by God's own hand;
She lived in the Garden of Eden with Adam, and through them sin first entered into man.

Sarah was the mother of nations, Abraham's lovely and dutiful wife;
In her attempt to assist God in His promise of a son, she would bring pain into her life.

Hagar was used in a despicable way by Sarah to obtain Abraham a son;
Resulting in arrogance and prideful ways, but her son was not the promised one!

Lot's wife was perhaps the saddest of all; worldliness was her biggest fault;
She will forever be remembered as one who looked back and turned to a pillar of salt.

Rebekah was loved by Isaac, and twin sons, Esau and Jacob they would share;
Isaac loved Esau, but she was partial to Jacob resulting in deceit, sorrow and despair.

Leah and Rachel were sisters who both loved Patriarch Jacob from the very start;
God honored each one as mothers in the history of Israel, but Rachel captured Jacob's heart.

Dinah was the daughter of Jacob and Leah, and she was sheltered, loved, and adored;
Curiosity and a pagan festival would cause her to be defiled, and her brothers' actions would be abhorred.

Jochebed was the faithful mother of a trio of children, whom God chose for His people to deliver;
Her faith would be rewarded when she chose to save her son, Moses, by placing him in the Nile River.

Miriam, the prophetess in joyful thanksgiving, with her timbrel led the women in song;
God had led them out of bondage in Egypt, and in the pages of history, she would always belong.

Rahab, the prostitute, would be part of God's plan by the assisting and hiding of the spies;
May we never judge others of their past sins when they have been justified in God's eyes.

Deborah was the only woman judge, highly respected and honored by all.
With insistence from Barak, she went into battle and watched all of their enemies fall.

"Where you go, I will go, where you lodge, I will lodge; your people and your God will be my own."
Ruth said these words to Naomi, and in Bethlehem awaited one of the greatest love stories ever known.

Hannah was the wife of Elkanah; she was barren and daily for a son she did pray;
Samuel was dedicated to the service of the Lord, and oh what an important part in history he would play.

Abigail was known for her wisdom when she stopped David's attack on her household;
When her evil husband refused food to the king and his men, her actions were prayerful and bold.

Bathsheba was the mother of Solomon when she became King David's wife;
But David's sin of adultery, deceit, and murder would cause his kingdom to forever have strife.

Jehosheba is known for courage and faith when she saved baby Joash from being killed;
It was through this great woman of old that prophecy of the lineage of David would be fulfilled.

Last but not least, Esther would be queen at just the right time to help save her people, the Jews;
An edict said to destroy them all, but through her God intervened, and today we still share the Good News.